THE
Farmer's Wife
SAMPLER QUILT
Coloring
Book

Color 70 Classic Quilt Designs from
Your Favorite Sampler Collection

LAURIE AARON HIRD
Illustrated by Missy Shepler

Fons&Porter
CINCINNATI, OHIO

INTRODUCTION

What you're holding in your hands is a collection of 70 blocks from *The Farmer's Wife Sampler Quilt* book specially selected and illustrated for you to infuse with your own sense of design and creativity. Coloring quilt blocks isn't an entirely new concept. For centuries, quilters have drawn up quilts on paper and colored in blocks to visualize what fabrics might blend or contrast best. But here, graphic designer Missy Shelper has filled these classic blocks with beautiful patterns, inspired by actual period fabric prints. With an artist's eye, she's turned the task of coloring quilt blocks into a rewarding and relaxing craft in its own right. What also makes this coloring book unique is that each design is printed in warm, sepia-tone ink on off-white pages. This not only speaks to the charming farmer's wife letters that play an essential role in the block book series, but gives your colorwork a harmonious look. Included in this book are 70 designs, seven overall quilts and nine blocks for each. Missy has done an outstanding job of rendering each block with an intricate, yet color-friendly mix of design elements, making it virtually impossible to pick a favorite. The book's square format serves as the perfect companion to the sampler quilt series and is intended for you to color and enjoy—no quilting or sewing required. Should your efforts inspire an actual quilting project, consider it a delightful bonus!

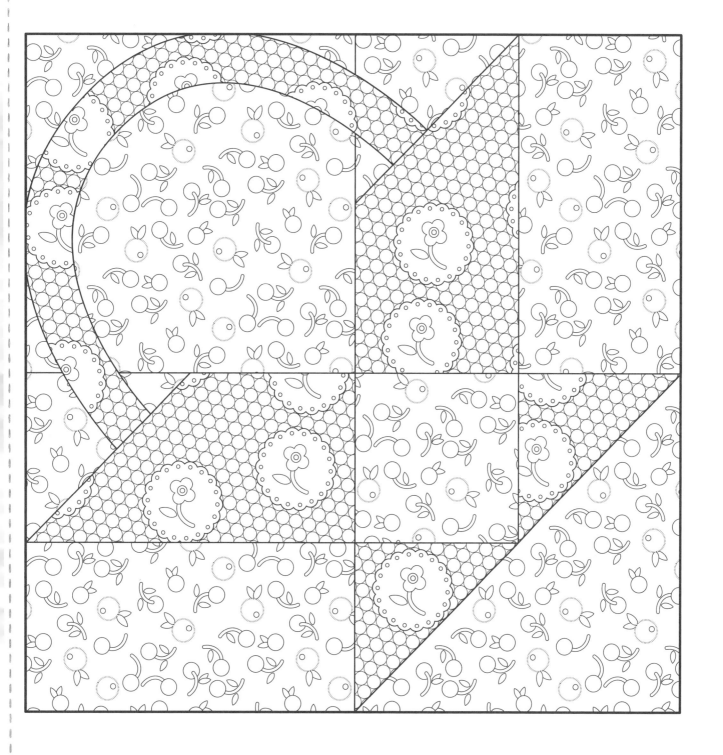

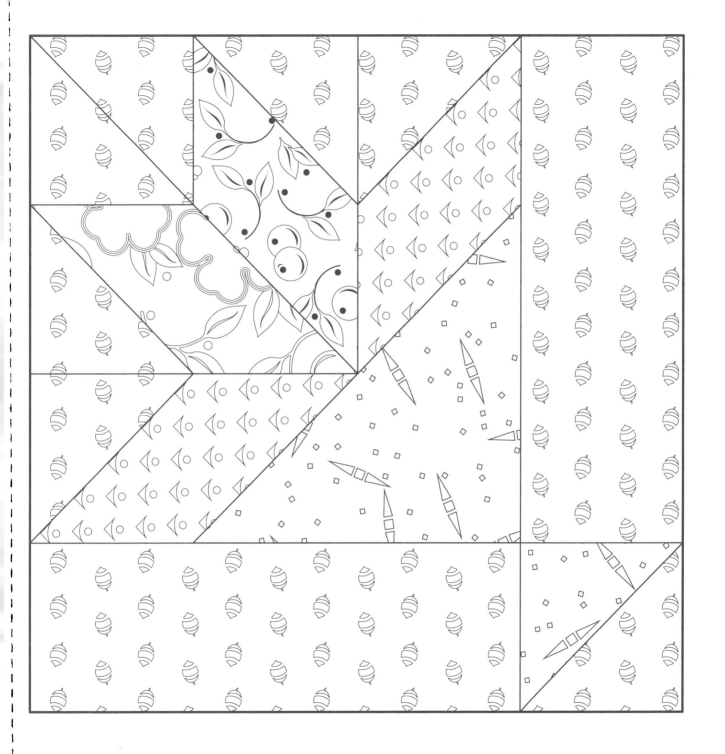

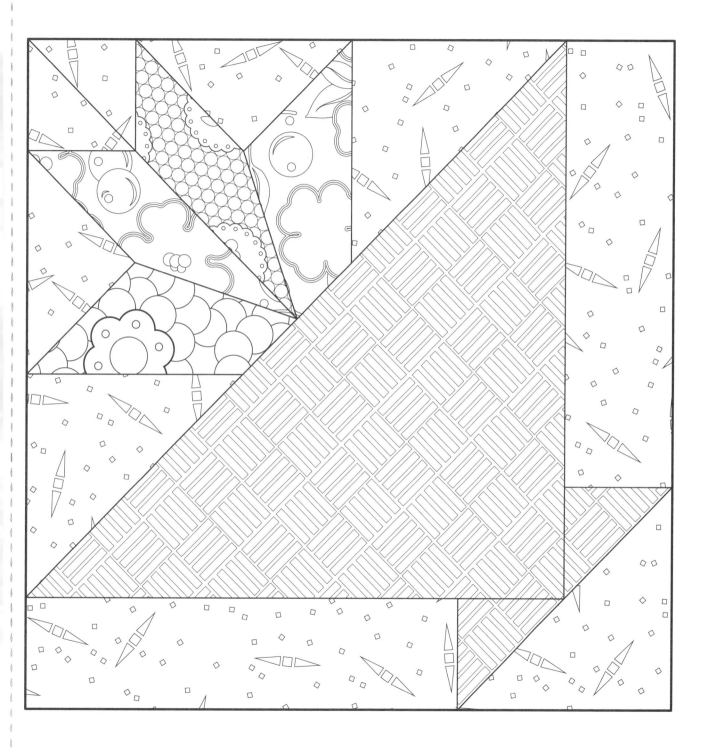

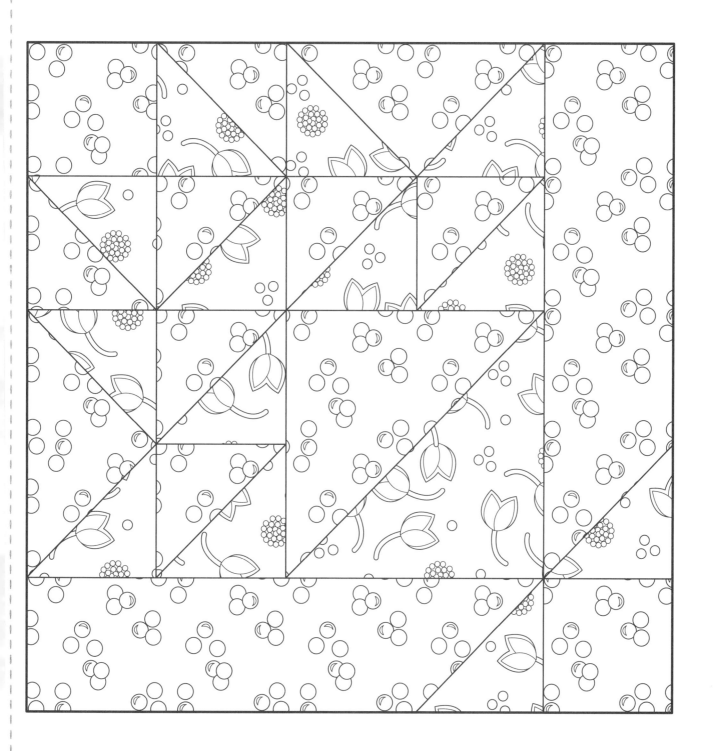

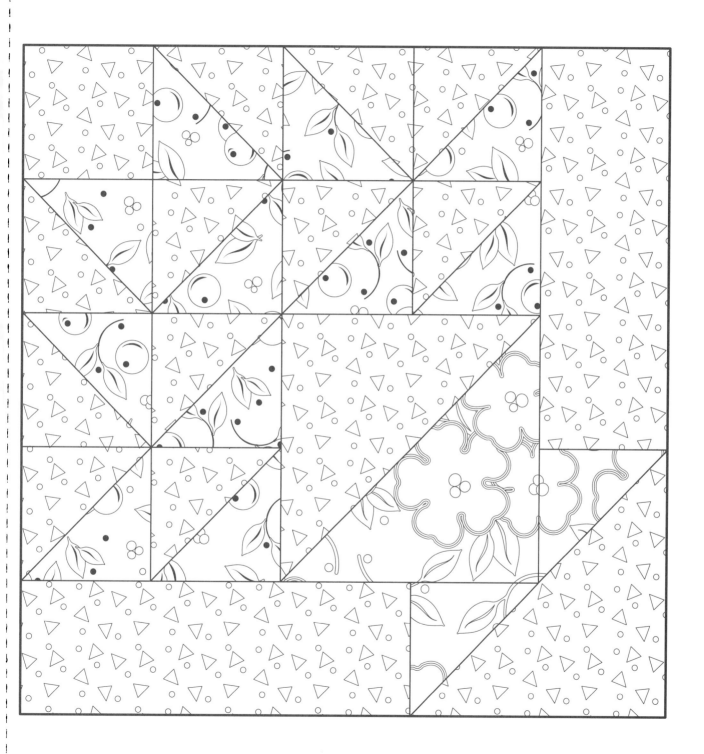

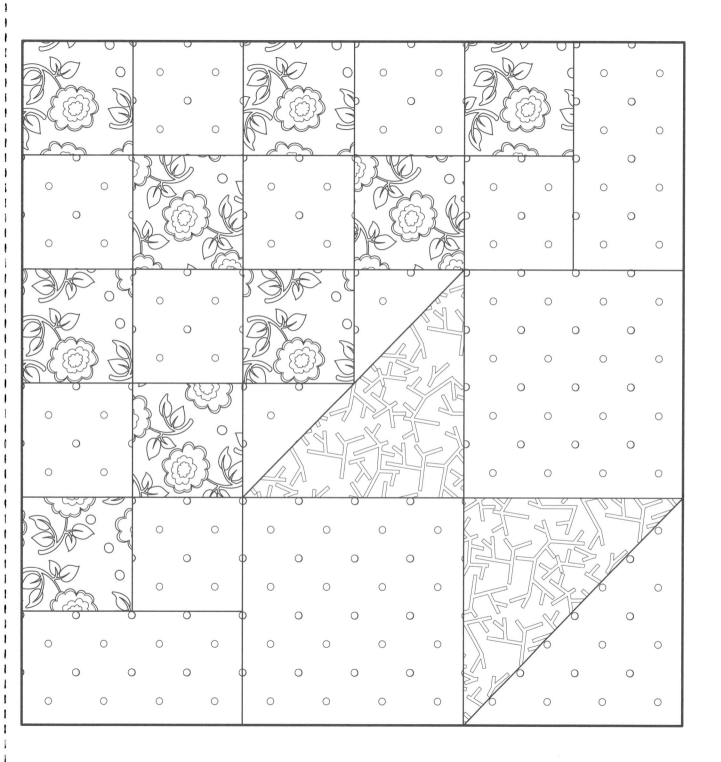

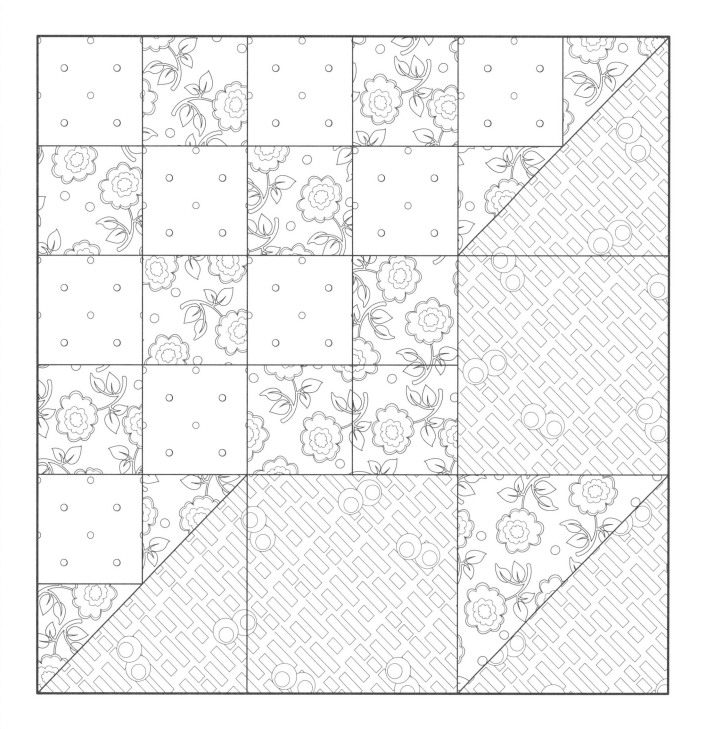

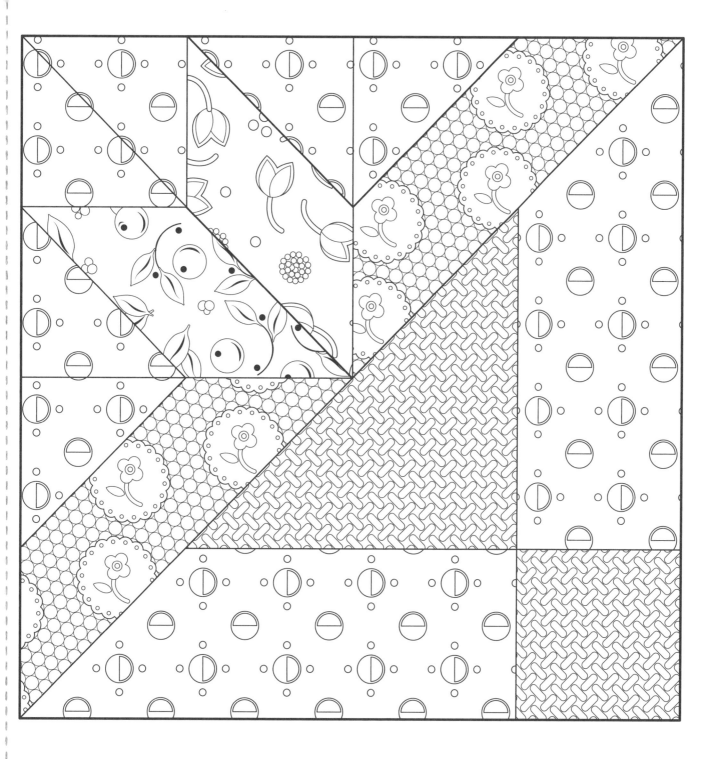

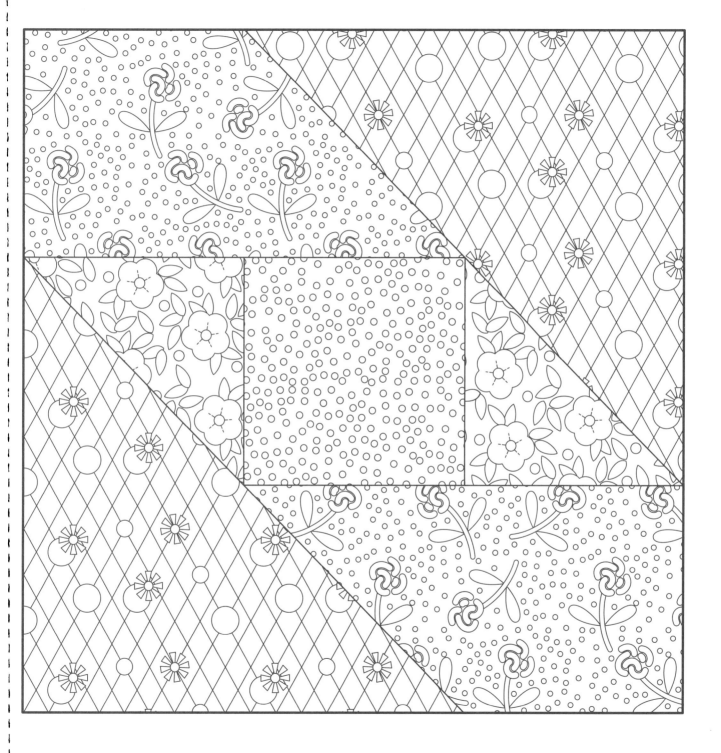

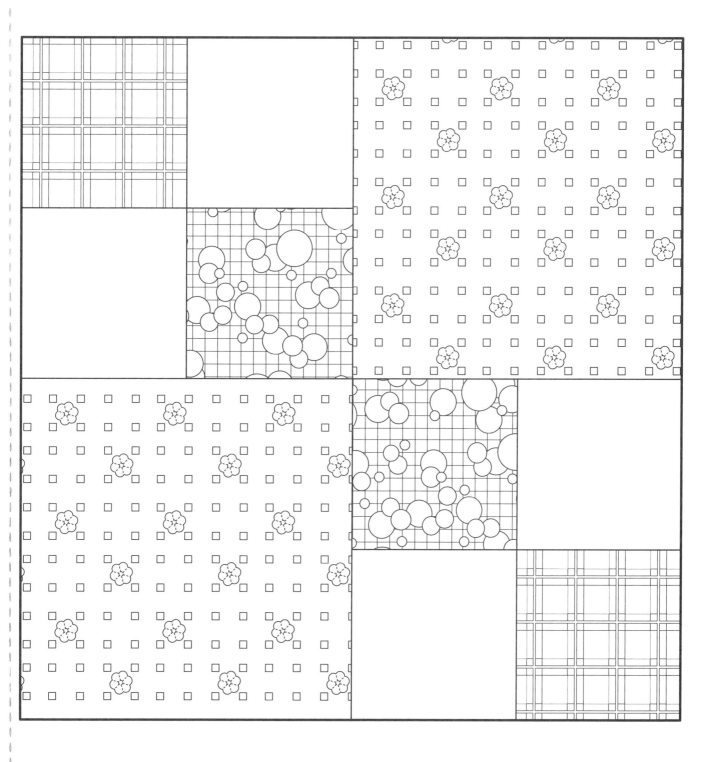

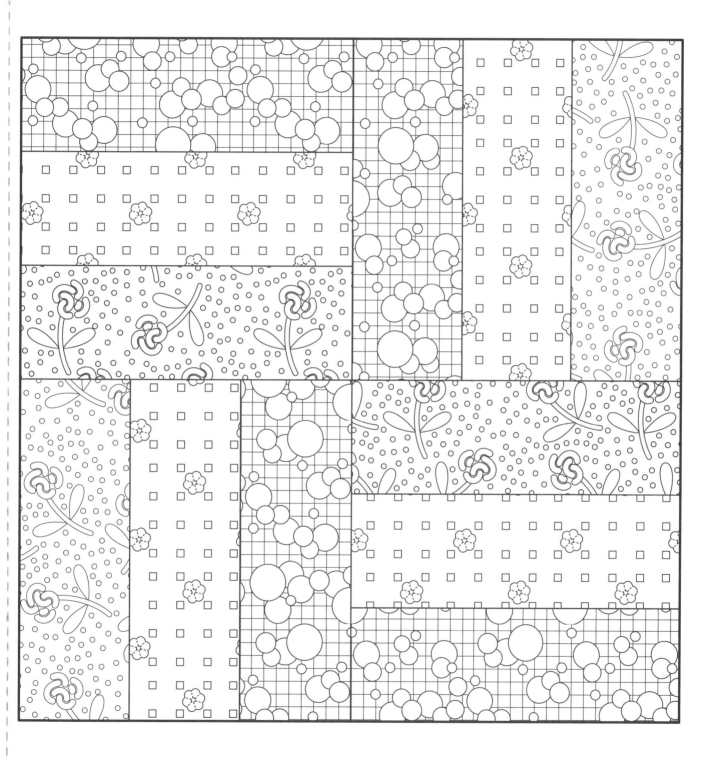

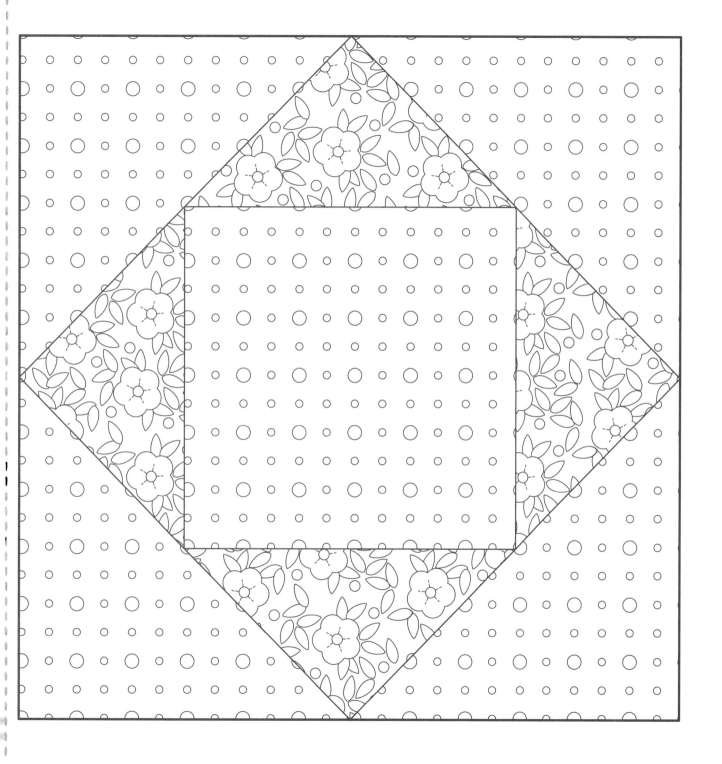

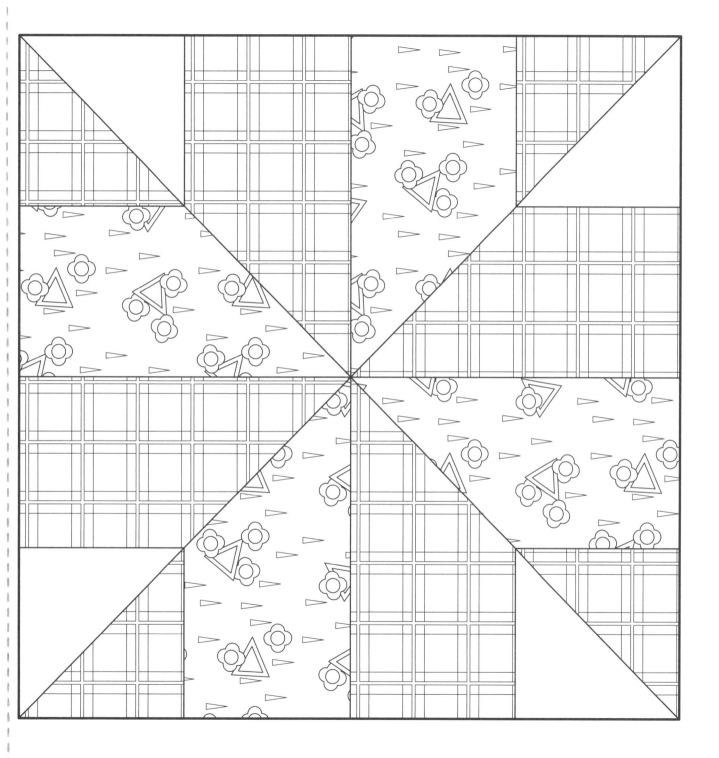

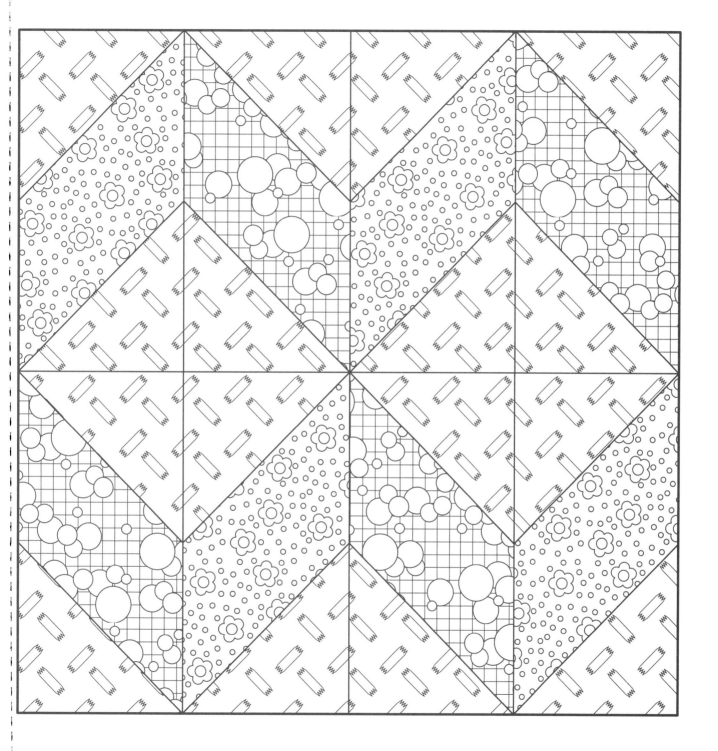

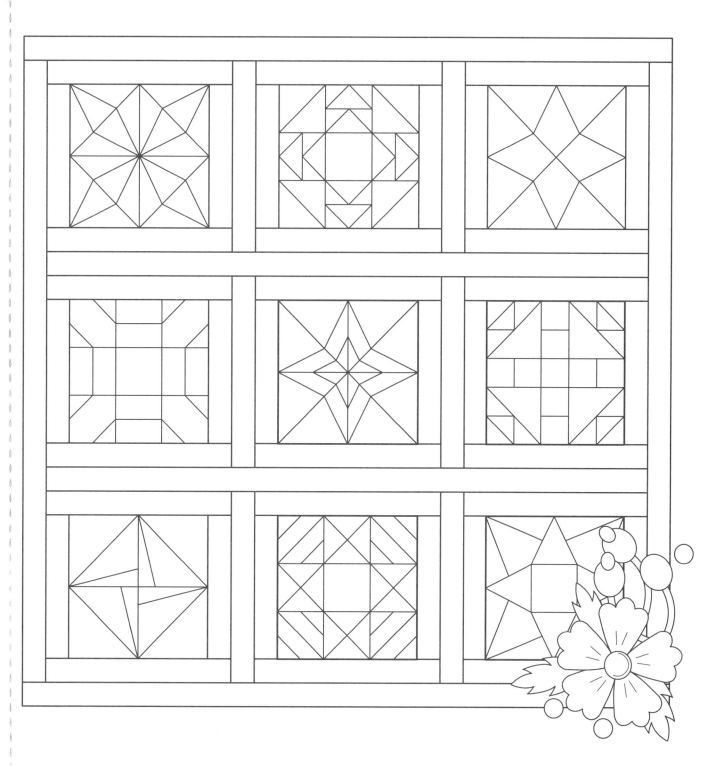

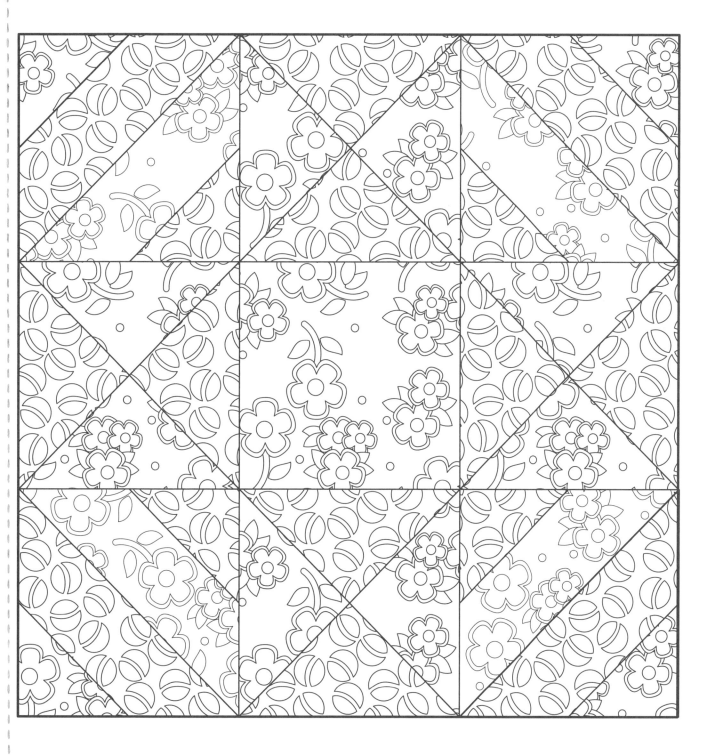

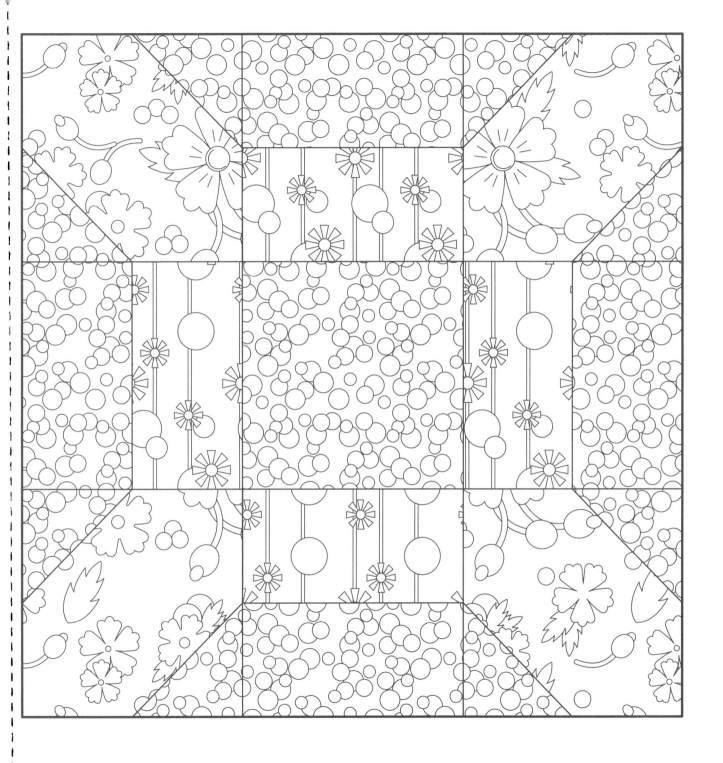

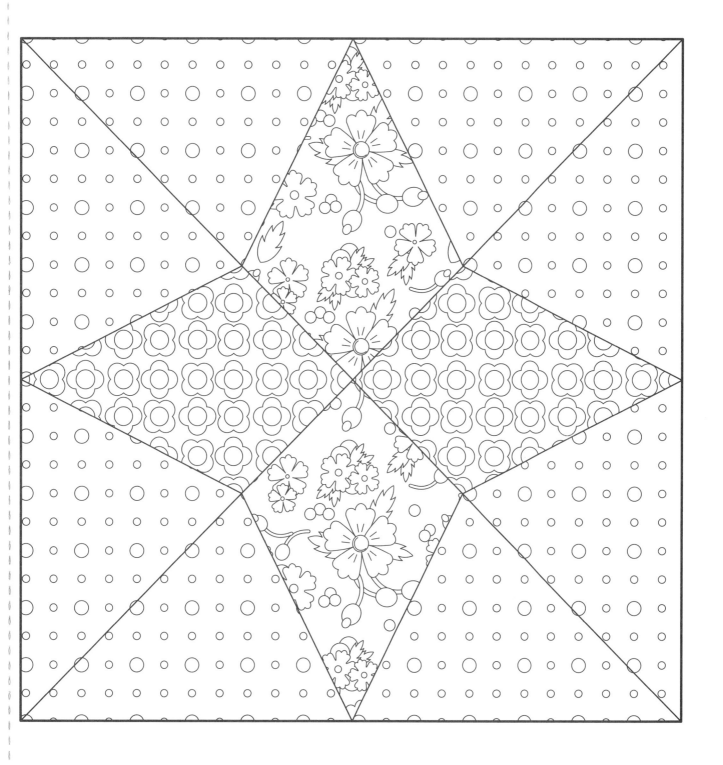

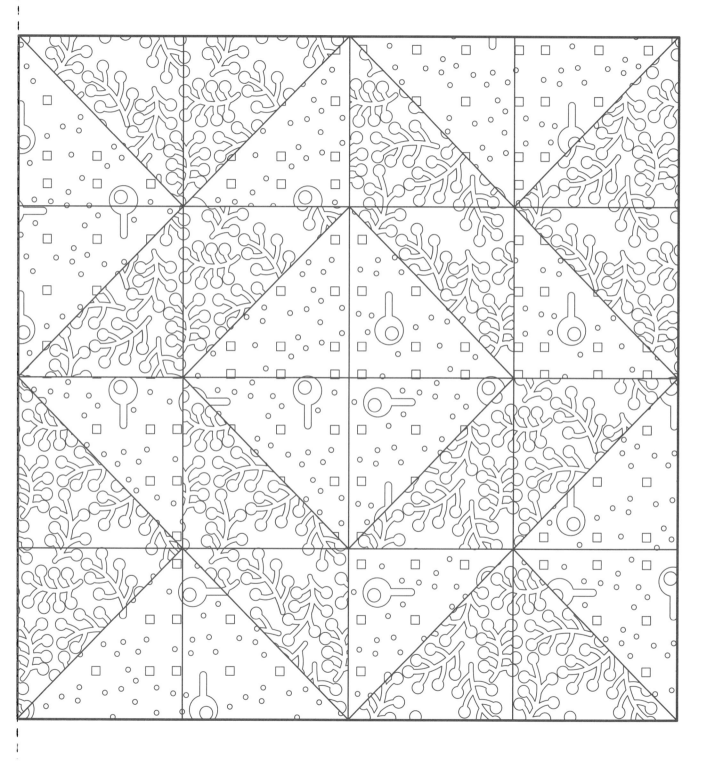

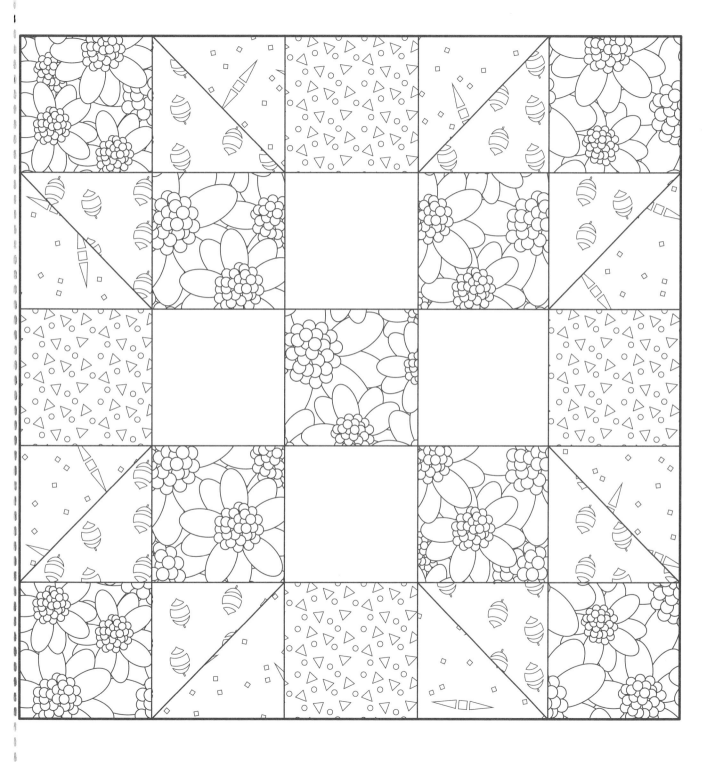

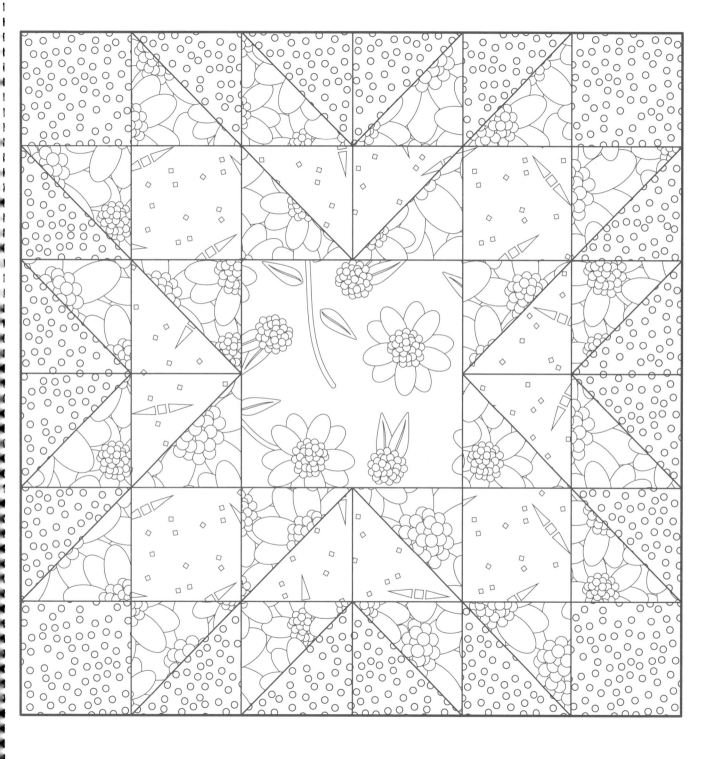

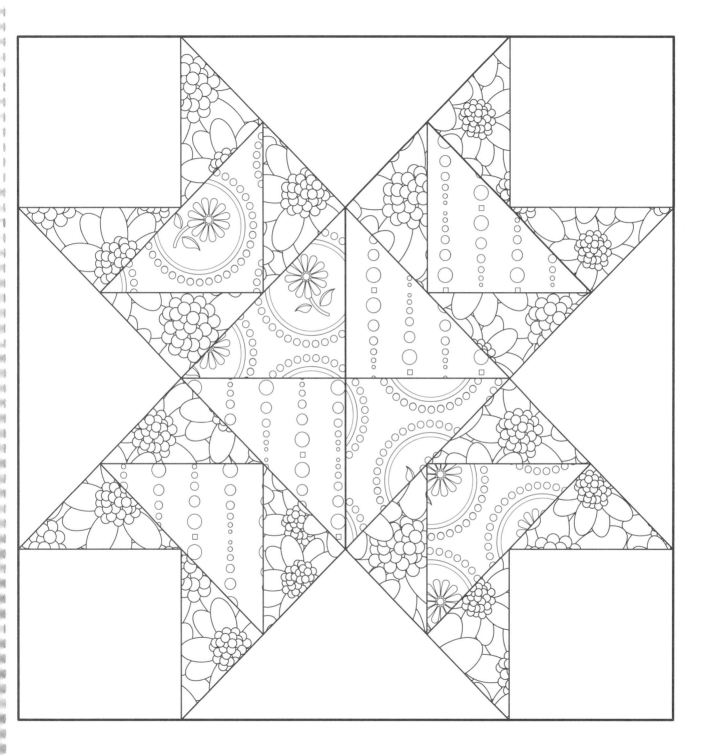

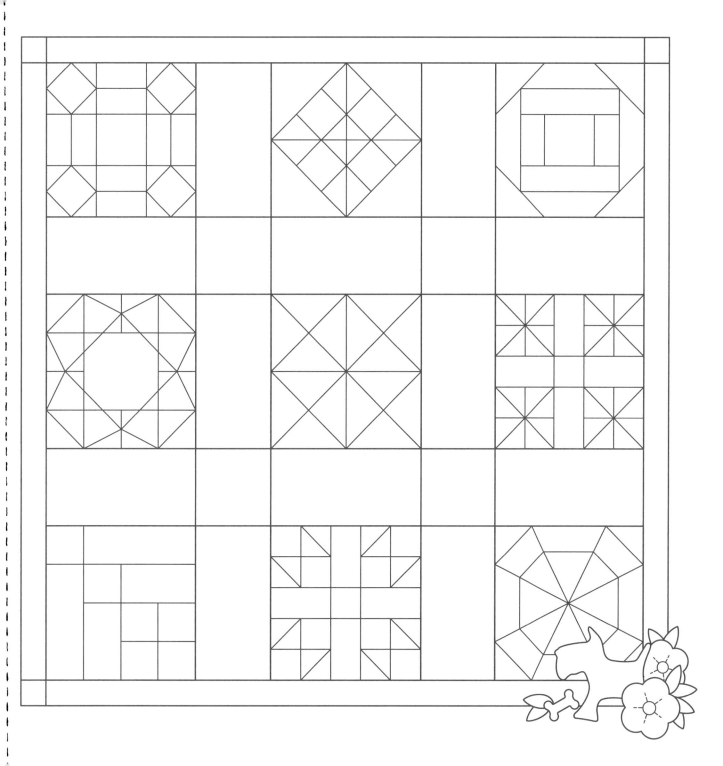

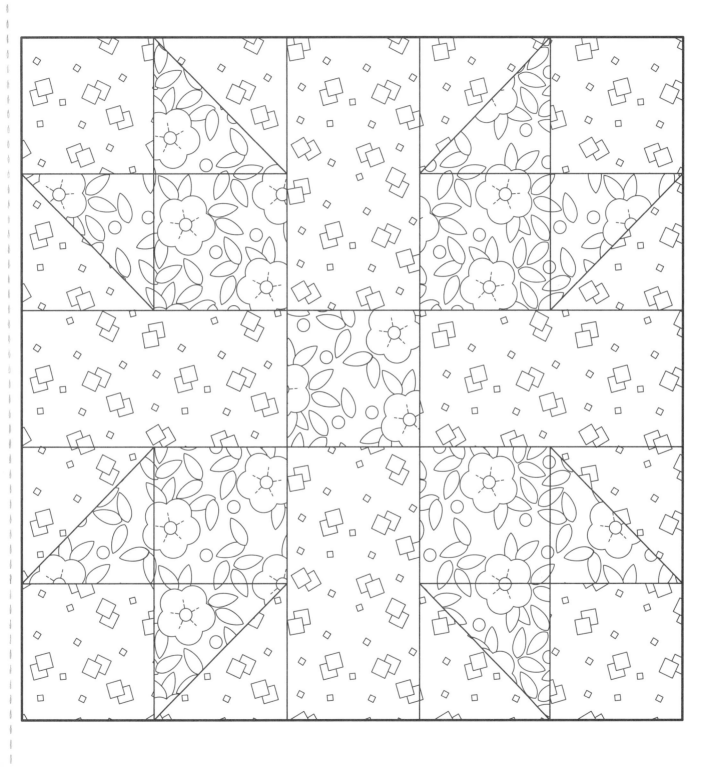

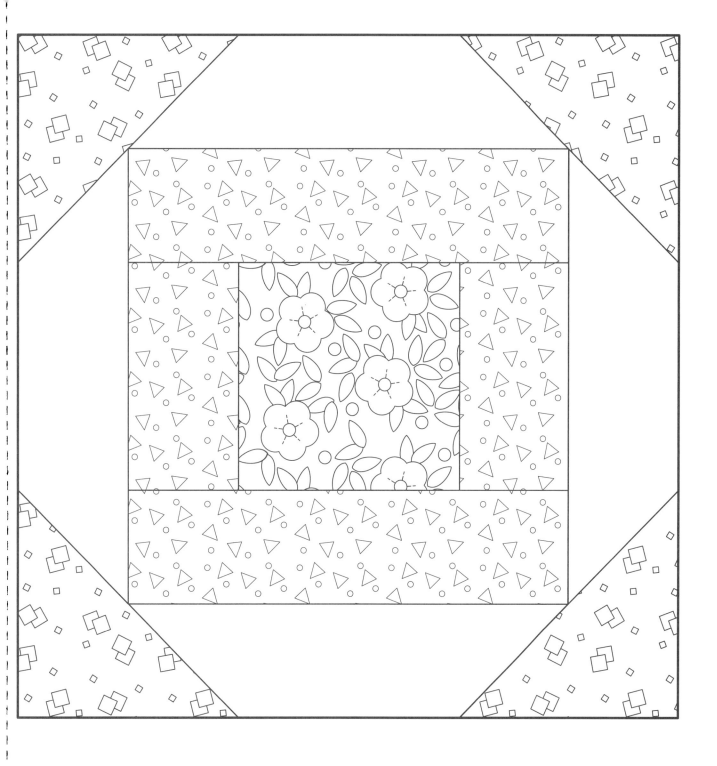

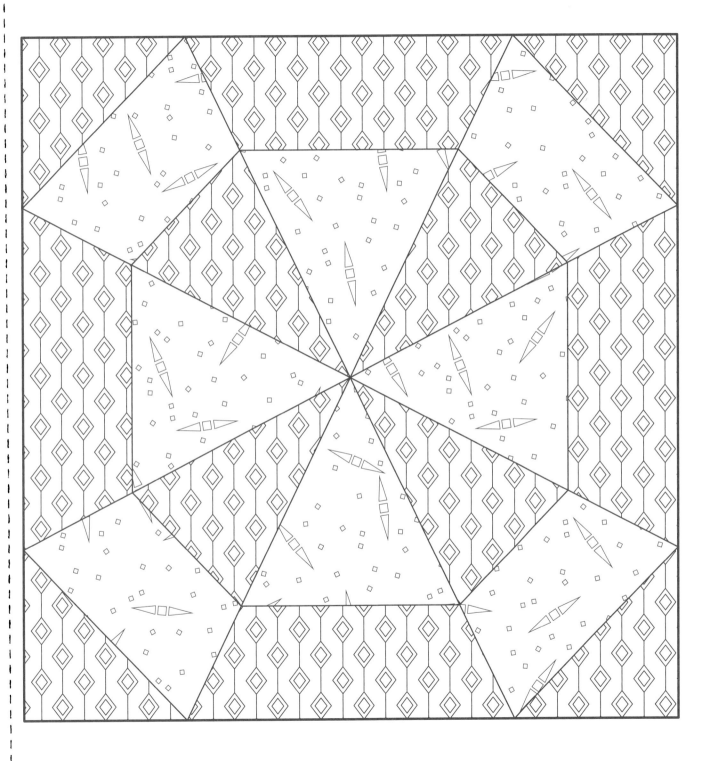

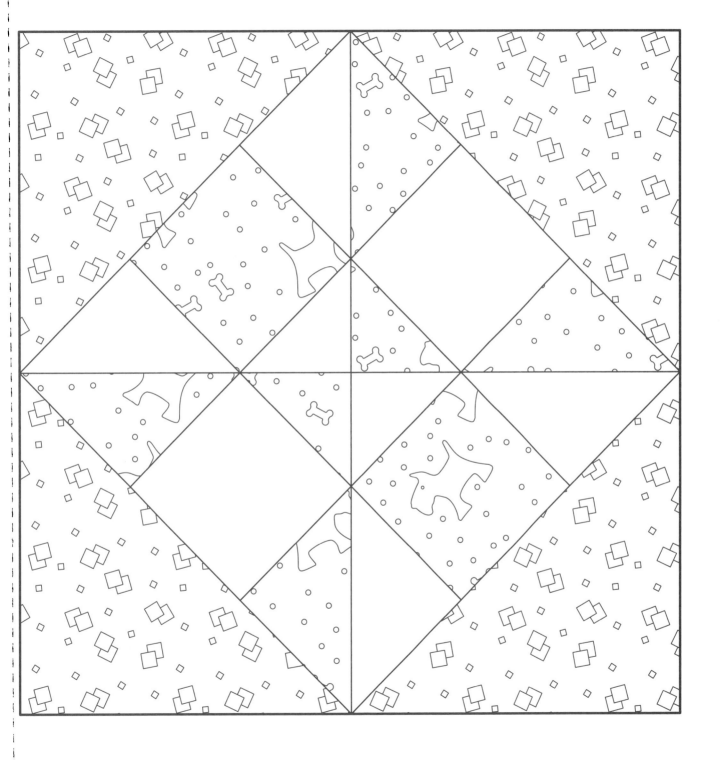

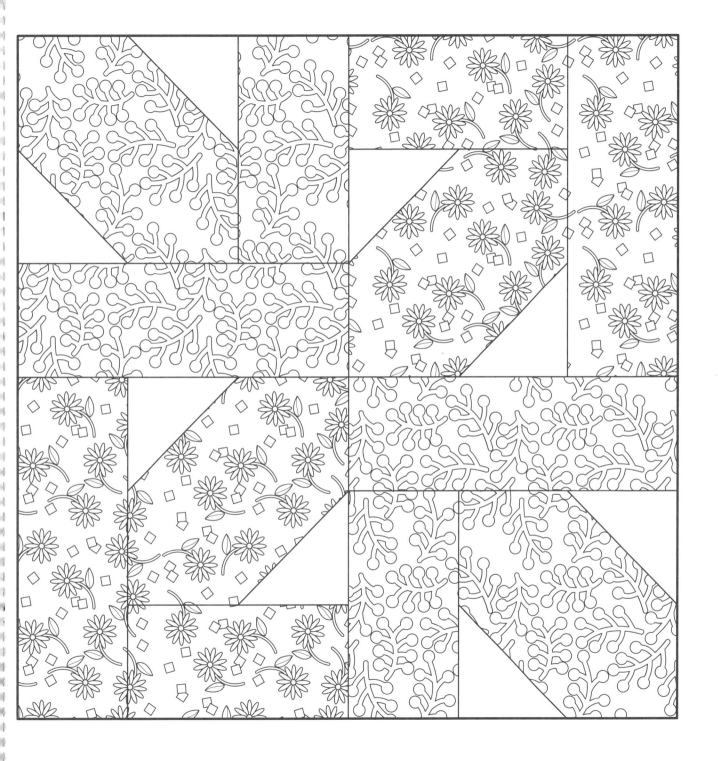

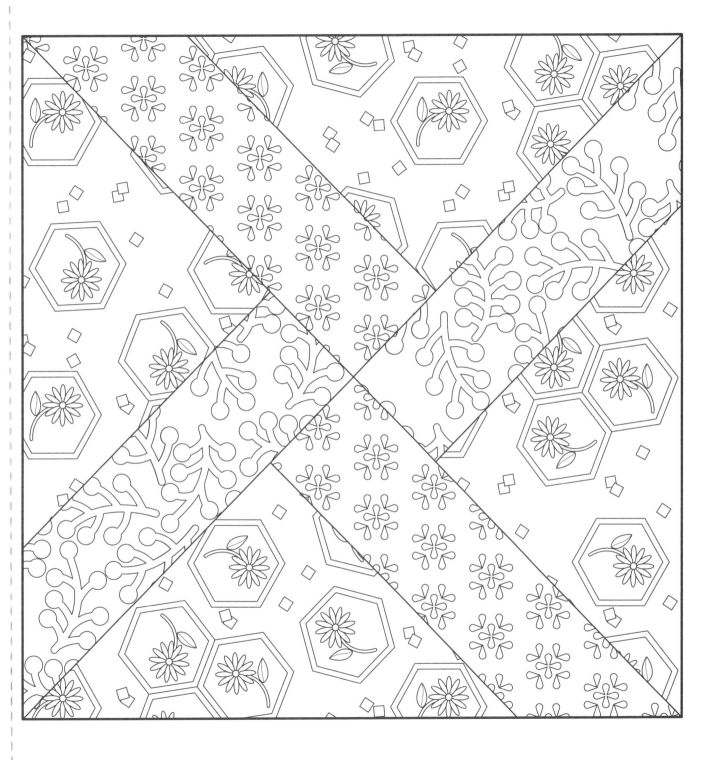

a content + ecommerce company

19 18 17 16 15   5 4 3 2 1

Distributed in Canada by Fraser Direct
100 Armstrong Avenue
Georgetown, ON, Canada L7G 5S4
Tel: (905) 877-4411

Distributed in the U.K. and Europe by
F&W MEDIA INTERNATIONAL
Pynes Hill Court, Pynes Hill, Rydon Lane, Exeter,
EX2 5SP, England
Tel: (+44) 1392 797680
E-mail: enquiries@fwmedia.com

Distributed in Australia by Capricorn Link
P.O. Box 704, S. Windsor NSW, 2756 Australia
Tel: (02) 4560 1600, Fax: (02) 4577 5288
E-mail: books@capricornlink.com.au

SRN: R0404
ISBN-13: 978-1-4402-4671-5

Edited by Amelia Johanson
Layout by Michelle Roy Kelly
Production coordinated by Jennifer Bass
Illustrations by Missy Shepler

If using markers, place a sheet of paper between pages to help prevent color from bleeding through to adjacent designs.

LAURIE AARON HIRD enjoys quilting, embroidery, and her porch view of the countryside from her home in the great Midwest. She is the author of *The Farmer's Wife Sampler Quilt* and *The Farmer's Wife 1930s Sampler Quilt* books.

MISSY SHEPLER is an illustrator, author, and designer with a home-based studio in central Illinois. She learned to sew a long time ago, by pushing a big plastic needle threaded with thick yarn through pre-punched sewing cards, and hasn't stopped stitching since. Missy has co-authored two books, contributed quilt designs and sewing patterns to many publications, and happily created more how-to illustrations than she can count. See more of her work online at MissyStitches.com.